SUPER CARS

LAMBORGHINI

HURACÁN

This Notebook Belongs To:

Henri

Date_____ Page_____

Date_____ Page_____

Date_____ Page_____

Date_____ Page_____

Date_____ Page_____

Date_____ Page_____

Date_____ Page_____

Date_____ Page_____

Date_____ Page_____

Date_____ Page_____

Date_____ Page_____

Date_____ Page_____

Date_____ Page_____

Date_____ Page_____

Date_____ Page_____

Date_____ Page_____

Date_____ Page_____

Date_____ Page_____

Date_____ Page_____

Date_____ Page_____

Date_____ Page_____

Date_____ Page_____

Date_____ Page_____

Date_____ Page_____

Date_____ Page_____

Date_____ Page_____

Date_____ Page_____

Date_____ Page_____

Date_____ Page_____

Date_____ Page_____

Date_____ Page_____

Date_____ Page_____

Date_____ Page_____

Date_____ Page_____

Date_____ Page_____

Date_____ Page_____

Date_____ Page_____

Date_____ Page_____

Date_____ Page_____

Date_____ Page_____

Date_____ Page_____

Date_____ Page_____

Date_____ Page_____

Date_____ Page_____

Date_____ Page_____

Date_____ Page_____

Date_____ Page_____

Date_____ Page_____

Date_____ Page_____

Date_____ Page_____

Date_____ Page_____

Date_____ Page_____

Date_____ Page_____

Date_____ Page_____

Date_____ Page_____

How do you like this notebook?
We value all feedback, Please leave a review
to help us improve the products on Amazon.
Thank you for sharing with us.

LAMBORGHINI NOTEBOOK

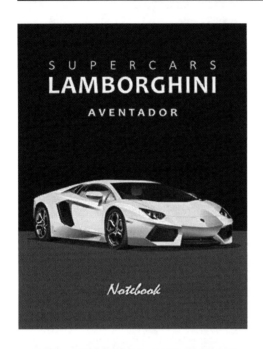
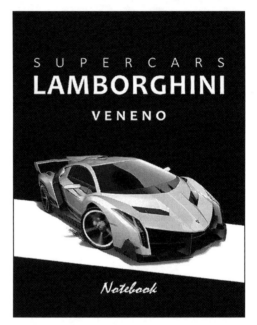
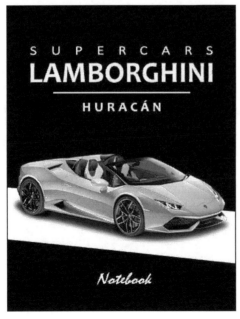

Made in the USA
Middletown, DE
04 November 2018